# SLEEPWALKER

*poems by*

# Linda K Sienkiewicz

*Finishing Line Press*
Georgetown, Kentucky

# SLEEPWALKER

Copyright © 2023 by Linda K Sienkiewicz
ISBN 979-8-88838-223-3 First Edition
All rights reserved under International and Pan-American Copyright Conventions. No part of this book may be reproduced in any manner whatsoever without written permission from the publisher, except in the case of brief quotations embodied in critical articles and reviews.

## ACKNOWLEDGMENTS

Blown Hollow: *Call & Response 3: Poets and Artists in Dialogue*
Elegy for a Son; Family Portrait: *Security Chapbook*
From Our House to Your House: *Mom Egg Review*; based on the poem by Jack Ridl
The Second Worst Thing: First Place in the Springfed Arts Poetry Contest 2021
Sleepwalker: *Almost Touching Anthology*
Solo Suite: Finalist for the Julia Darling Poetry Prize 2022
Too Soon: *Prairie Schooner*
What Every Mother Hopes For: *Mobius: A Journal for Social Change*

With special thanks to the Detroit literary community for their support, and in particular Terry Blackhawk, Diane DeCillis, Diana Dinverno, Cindy Frenkel, Joy Gaines Friedler, Mary Jo Firth Gillett, Jeffrey Hermann, Melinda LaPere, Nancy Owen Nelson, Jack Ridl, Lucinda Sabino, Denise Sedman, Russell Thorburn, and Carolyn Walker.

Publisher: Leah Huete de Maines
Editor: Christen Kincaid
Cover Art: Linda K Sienkiewicz
Author Photo: Emilee Freyman, emileerosefilms.com
Cover Design: Elizabeth Maines McCleavy

Order online: www.finishinglinepress.com
also available on amazon.com

Author inquiries and mail orders:
Finishing Line Press
PO Box 1626
Georgetown, Kentucky 40324
USA

# Table of Contents

Moon and No Stars ................................................................. 1

What Every Mother Hopes For ............................................. 2

Gone: A Dream ....................................................................... 4

Family Portrait ........................................................................ 5

Sleepwalker .............................................................................. 6

Elegy For Another Son .......................................................... 7

From Our House to Your House .......................................... 8

Little Cuts ................................................................................ 9

Erasure ................................................................................... 10

The Second Worst Thing ..................................................... 11

Blown Hollow ....................................................................... 12

Clean ...................................................................................... 13

Lucky Boy .............................................................................. 14

Watering ................................................................................ 16

After Ten Years My Late Son Visits .................................... 17

Homemade ............................................................................ 18

Solo Suite ............................................................................... 19

Jump Drive ............................................................................ 21

Too Soon ................................................................................ 22

# MOON AND NO STARS
*by Derek I. Sienkiewicz (1979 – 2011)*

Imagine a night with a moon and no stars.
Oh how brightly a reflection does shine,
But lonely its path, like this heart of mine.

It rises and falls alone in the night,
The course that it travels and shadows it casts,
A moon with no stars; those nights never last.

But brilliant against a backdrop of stars,
The larger it grows with an infinite friend.
Lumines in the dark; those nights never end.

A moon with no stars is no moon at all
Like a soul with no peace is sentenced to roam.
A moon with no stars; a moon with no home.

This is my scope, which I use to see,
And you are my moon,
And you are my stars.

## WHAT EVERY MOTHER HOPES FOR
*from the book "Desolation Island" by Patrick O'Brian*

Imagine a boy first class, age eleven,
helping the crew hoist cannons, provisions,
anchors, cables, even the forge overboard
while the pumps belch out a ton of water
a minute, and the sea throws it back.

In the sleet of dark December, mission failed,
the crew works a fothering-sail beneath
the thousand-and-fifty ton warship,
but can't stay the leak. The starboard
pump-chain breaks. Water fills the hold,

seventeen feet, rises above the gunwale.
The larboard pump fails. Men hide,
nurse crushed fingers. It's an unlucky ship
they say, haunted by the two-headed fetch
of a murdered sheriff's man.

Two hundred years before my son joins
the Navy and later takes his life, before
ships are nuclear powered, a boy on the swirling
deck sobs convulsively as even the rats jump ship.
The captain says any man who wants

can leave, and Godspeed. Bawling officers,
poxed lubbers, toothless scurvied
seaman, most of them unable to swim,
raid the spirit room, loot the cabins,
claw and kill for the boats. The boy

wipes his nose on his sleeve, stands by
the captain's side. He tells the boy
she'll be lighter now, says she'll sail.
I like this story. I like this story because
even as something inside the captain dies

as he watches the last of them go astern:
*the dark struggling mass
in the icy water as those in the sea
fight to get into the boats and those
in the boats fight to keep them out*

and that's not the worst of it—
stranded on Desolation Island
with scurvy, a broken rudder, no forge
to rebuild the frigate—I like this story
because the boy comes home.

## GONE: A DREAM

I run through the rooms of the house,
each door is smaller than the last
until I have to crawl into my bedroom.
I hear my son run up the stairs.
I slam the door, see myself
in a mirror, then turn away.

My son talks to me through the door,
upset about something, again,
and I'm angry, again, because he'll be
late for summer school, bad enough
that he's in summer school.

The phone interrupts. *Hello?
Hello?* I ask but no one answers
until a voice finally shouts
*Well, lady, you gonna change
phone companies or what?*

I tell my son to get going.
From the upstairs window I watch
him back his Jeep from the driveway
into the middle of the front lawn.
He flings his guitar from the trunk
followed by all the toys he'd asked
me to save: Tonka trucks, LEGO
bricks, trading cards, spinning
ninjas, hockey skates, pucks.

I shout from the window *Why?*
He glares back at me
from the car as he drives away.
A black sedan screeches past.
My son slams his brakes. I want to
jump from the window after him
but I'm tangled in the curtains.

# FAMILY PORTRAIT

The eldest son stands far left, hair tamed
in a U MISS baseball cap that his parents
give up trying to make him remove. His
feet turn toward his mother, but his eyes
are distant, hands fisted, presence elsewhere.
The middle boy has passed him in height
and stands balanced on the outside edges
of his shoes. Later he'll punch his brother
in the back over a soda. The youngest
is a girl in a red plaid jumper, tangled rope
of blond hair over one eye, head tilted,
weight on her left foot, right pointed,
ready to arabesque across the room
earning her brothers' sneers.
Mother and Father hold opposite ends, smiling.
It is all as should be. Tomorrow,
the party balloons will loll under the table
and the score of the football game
on the television behind them
will be in the standings. But for now,
the children oblige
the photographer's count to three.

## SLEEPWALKER

Second to the right and then
straight on till morning,
my son wanders alone
in another place, a different time,
turning the invisible pages
of a happily-ever-after fairy tale.
I sleep in my tennis shoes,
one ear tuned for the nonsensical jabber
that precedes his vacant-eyed walk
down the hallway to the stairs.

I wonder if he's searching for
some once-upon-a-time land
where fairy mothers give three wishes,
not a scolding when the day gets long.
I fear he might decide to stay
lost in the Land of Giants, or follow
the town musicians to Bremen
and never want to come back.

Each night I give him my kiss
to wear on a chain around his neck.
I wish I had a magic mirror
to let me step into his dreams
or a wooden shoe to rock him in,
sailing on the misty sea.
Up all night, I am
on the other side of his journey.

## ELEGY FOR ANOTHER SON

I imagine you in the parking lot,
so much a man at age eighteen,
youthful impatience and honor
to defend. Was it easy to be brave
after midnight and five beers?

Did you see the Pontiac pull up
or the gunman leaning out the window?
The girl whose attention you fought for
wasn't with you, but she may have felt
a chill up her back when the bullet

hit your head. At that moment, your mother
may have felt a thud deep in her womb.
I remember my miscarriage years ago,
all the blood I couldn't hold back
slowly spreading across the bathroom tile.

That death was not like yours.
I never knew the baby I lost,
but the boy I birthed a year later
grew to be your friend,
attend your wake and hug your mother.

I never met you. That doesn't mean
I was able to swallow my scrambled eggs
when the Morning Press
spelled the details of your death,
or that words don't cry

out of me in the middle of the night,
or that I turn away when I see
your smile on the memorial card
taped to my son's mirror—
I can't hold him back either.

## FROM OUR HOUSE TO YOUR HOUSE

A blue wave is rising, or maybe it's red,
depending on your source. We are afraid
of Russia, not that they will nuke us but
rather melt our brains with microwaves.
We pose on our IKEA couch. We
love our ergonomic furniture.
We wear jeggings and organic hemp-fiber
t-shirts. Our hair is messy on purpose.
Blue Apron dinners arrive weekly at
our door. We smile when we cook because
we drink. We drink because the future doesn't look
sunny from where we sit. We hire a dog
whisperer for our unruly Corgi.
Our eldest child is missing from the picture.
He will always be missing. Our second
eldest moved back home. We're not sure
when he'll leave. Our grandchildren play
Minecraft on their iPads. We post their pictures
on Instagram with our smart phones. We believe
in sustainability, medical
marijuana and Hulu. Happiness
is overrated. We pray for a blue wave.
In the spring we may consider Canada.

## LITTLE CUTS

When I was a girl
every body
of water harbored
an alligator,
every darkness
hid hands, every knife
promised a cut.

The wind on the trail
pushes me back.
My hips ache,
dust fills my eyes
and in my ears
an endless loop
of words play
while I pedal—
*You were never there
for me.*

Maybe what I thought
was sacrifice
you considered a given.

And what
you considered
sacrifice
I couldn't give.

## ERASURE

Your great grandfather was a sailor.
Small and nimble he climbed
the riggings and set the sails,

bananas from Africa to Finland.
He built a ship
in a smoky glass bottle.

When I was a girl I turned it
around and around—how
did he get that ship inside?

His weathered arms
creased his sail ship tattoos.
He'd be proud you served

in the Navy even though
you weren't and later paid someone
to laser your nautical tattoos.

That must have hurt. You didn't
always want your picture taken
and one time tried to tear yourself

from our family albums. You,
hiding behind a box of Cheerios,
You, hiding behind a birthday card.

Your great grandfather hid
behind thick glasses, talked little.
Some people are private.

You asked me to keep
your poems a secret. I'm sorry
I broke my promise.

# THE SECOND WORST THING

on the day
we found you
the police made us leave

your apartment
*Crime scene,* they said

though it wasn't

your father and I sat
on the hard rubber treads
of the stairs in the hallway

the landlady fretted

I made a phone call
or two

the police took
your laptop
your notebooks

I don't know what else—

and then
you

The next worst thing—
your aunt running
down the sidewalk
arms waving
screaming

and later
your eighty-nine year-old
grandmother
crying
in my lap

## BLOWN HOLLOW

I can't tell you the bad thoughts
I have, how antagonistic I feel,
can't eat or sleep, hollowed dry,
punkish, marooned. I run out
in the rain, shake my fist at the sky,
scrawny hydrangea, ransacked
bird feeder, then drop to my knees
in the slick grass. My son is dead,
my granddaughter's friend has leukemia,
a Navy vet comes to our food pantry with
stage four stomach cancer and can't get
a doctor to see her. Another client sleeps
in a storage unit, his home of twenty years
repossessed, and a boy loses hot lunch
on his birthday because his mother owes
the school nine bucks, twenty-five thousand
people are missing in the Bahamas
and don't get me started on Puerto Rico:
the head of FEMA indicted on ten felonies.
This paper cut on my finger
makes me want to weep.

## CLEAN

We return to Ohio to empty your apartment.
Pictures of Marilyn and Sinatra on your walls,
the pre-lit Christmas tree I gave you
two years ago, outside on your patio.
Your fridge, immaculate, save for a magnet
on the door—your young niece
in a pink ballet costume. Your laptop, scrubbed.
Six drained wine bottles on the counter
and we can't find the key
for the '81 Corvette we didn't know you had.
I sprain my back trying to lift
a duffle bag loaded with old magazines.

The autopsy report comes back clean, only
mild arterial buildup. Hereditary.

## LUCKY BOY

You said you weren't sure
        one more day   and
        you might break down
  you didn't want to be
     a burden
       feared the unexamined life
            wasn't worth living
talked about the illuminati
        the rich taking over the world
        and began to write poetry

you bought a ticket to Egypt
        your ten-year plan included
            making a million

you sounded drunk
        on the phone
            one day
       ridiculing on another
wouldn't answer
       my call the next
then blocked my number
      after I said
           you were lucky

you misread me
        lucky boy
your friends loved you
but you couldn't
            feel

I feared visiting
>    worried
>        about what I'd find

The last time I saw you
>    alive
at your grandmother's
>            you tried to open a bottle
>    of wine with a paring knife
>    and played with
>        your toddler niece

She made you laugh
Everyone said
>    your laugh
>        could fill a room

## WATERING

My grandson waters the bricks.
I had hoped he would water
my flowers but he prefers
the patio and sidewalk,
watching the cement darken.

He hands me the empty
watering can. I carry it
to the hose for a refill
then lug it back to him.

Cold water sloshes
onto my shoes and legs.
There must be another way
but he's happy and busy

so I refill the can over
and again. What else is there?
He tells me all birds cry
except penguins.

*They live in the South Pole, Nana.*
*If they cry, their tears freeze.*

## AFTER TEN YEARS MY LATE SON VISITS

He parks his Hummer in the driveway,
comes in the back door.
*How's it goin', Moms?*

I say, *As well as can be.*
*You know.*

He says, *I know.*

I say, *Do you miss me?*

He says he misses
his Egyptian cotton sheets.

I offer him pot roast,
his favorite.

He says he quit eating.
Just gave it up.

I ask if he's cold.
He looks cold,
too thin. *I worry*
*about you.*
*What's it like?*
*Are you still sad?*

He says, *You don't have to*
*worry anymore.*

I say, *I can't stop. A mother just can't.*
*I wish I would have told you*
*that. There are so many things*
*I wish I would have told you.*

He says, *You can tell me*
*now. I'll listen.*

## HOMEMADE

Grandma Elsie knitted mittens and booties
tied with pompoms, an expression of love,
year after year. The wool warmed my hands
even when soggy with snow.
Some kid at the bus stop laughed at my
multicolored mittens. I wore them anyway,
one pair stuffed inside another.
I patched the soles of the slippers
and saved the soft white booties
Elsie knitted for my firstborn.

Both Elsie and firstborn are gone.
I wonder if my grandchildren
will save the face masks
with purple flowers, butterflies
and super heroes that I sewed for them.
The stakes are higher now
for grandmothers.

## SOLO SUITE

Linden's cello sighs
with each bow stroke
across the gut strings,
*Solo Suite Number Three*
in C major.
His head drops,
his eyes close,
his hand dances.
The cello weeps,
sighs, trills
and moans.

I hear you
in the sad
unhurried
depths.
Transported
from the audience
to sudden witness
in another time,
I see your hand
suspended
in the air
above your chest,
fingers frozen,
eyes closed,
your throat
tightly wrapped,
imagine your
last breath
in the final sigh

before you asked
death to take you.
I wanted
to push
your arm down,
beg please,
tell me, son,
what I see
isn't so,
what I hear
isn't
my own weeping.

# JUMP DRIVE

The cops picked him and his buddies up for loitering
at the Burger King on Walton. They gave him a hard time,

not believing Ignatius was his middle name, yet praised
him as the only teen who answered *Yes sir. No sir.*

As a boy he raided my jewelry drawer looking for gold
chains and beads so he could dress like his hero Mr. T,

other times, walked beside me through the grocer's
wearing red tights and a cape with a magic marker S.

We laughed about his twelfth birthday when I caught
my sweater on fire lighting the cake candles.

He and the sanctimonious boys across the street always
got into it, taunting each other and swiping basketballs.

He'd tell me about the lectures in high school law, but
failed the class because he couldn't take notes while listening.

Hearing his voice on that first call from boot camp at Great
Lakes Naval Center made me cry and that made him cry.

When he was stationed in Crete, a Greek teenager gave him
the red, white and blue leather jacket off his back.

The Navy praised his "rock-solid" performance
serving his helicopter squadron during

Operation Southern Watch over Iraqi no-fly zones.
I saved the letter. He never talked about it.

For Mother's Day, he filled a jump drive with every single
recording ever made by The Doors, my last gift from him.

## TOO SOON

I pour my third glass of Merlot
and address a sympathy card.
The cat leaps up, bats her foam ball
under my feet: this is rapture.
The dog rips into a beef-basted
chew bone: this is bliss. The whole room
stinks like dead cow but it's nice
to have content animals. My father's
girlfriend's sister died yesterday. Heavy
smoker, stole stranger's cigarette butts
from ashtrays to keep her habit.
I can't get used to saying *father's girlfriend.*
They're tennis partners who live together.
Sleep together too, I imagine.
The dog vomits a rawhide strip.
It's nice to vomit and be content.
There's only one time that I ever feel
so animal, so immersed in the joy
of the moment, even if painful,
and that's during sex. My husband lolls
in bed, I walk downstairs, naked under
my robe, still faintly buzzed.
Once you let go, the body takes over
and nothing matters— not cigarettes,
wine, *I'm sorry for your loss,*
the Black Hawk my son will fly
over Afghanistan and certainly not the alarm
which brings tomorrow too soon.

**RESOURCES**

If you have struggled with thoughts of suicide, or have lost a loved one to suicide, please know you are not alone.

If you are in crisis, call 988 or text TALK to 741-741 Available 24-7 Support resources can be found at the American Foundation for Suicide Prevention at afsp.org:

> When we stand together and express our emotions, we begin to heal. When we come together and talk, we are less lonely. We hear our own questions and concerns voiced aloud by others, and feel a sense of comfort that someone understands. The overwhelming intensity of our painful thoughts and emotions are diminished when spoken and shared. Healing is not a linear progression and our loss is not meant to be 'overcome,' but rather integrated into our lives as loss survivors.

Additional links:
American Association of Suicidology: *suicidology.org*
American Psychiatric Association: *finder.psychiatry.org*
Compassionate Friends: *compassionatefriends.org*
National Alliance on Mental Health: *nami.org*

Linda K. Sienkiewicz is an author, poet, artist and blogger. Her short stories, poems, essays and art have been published in numerous anthologies and literary journals, such as *Prairie Schooner, Permafrost, Clackamas Literary Review, Paterson Review, New Ohio Review, The MacGuffin* and *Spoon River Poetry Review*. Her essay, "My Horrible Celebrity Crush," appears in *Idol Talk: Women Writers on the Teenage Infatuations that Changed Their Lives*, published by McFarland. Her debut novel, *In the Context of Love*, was a finalist for multiple awards. She is the recipient of a poetry chapbook award from *Heartlands Today* and a Pushcart Prize nomination. Sienkiewicz has authored three other chapbooks: *Postcard of a Naked Man*; *Dear Jim*; and *Security*. She wrote and illustrated a children's picture book, *Gordy and the Ghost Crab*, published in 2020. She is a member of Detroit Working Writers, Detroit Writers Guild, Poetry Society of Michigan, Michigan Poets, Springfed Arts and the Society of Children's Book Writers and Illustrators. Connect with her at LindaKSienkiewicz.com

www.ingramcontent.com/pod-product-compliance
Lightning Source LLC
Chambersburg PA
CBHW022129090426
42743CB00008B/1065